Becoming

Poems for Awakening the Soul

Amanda L. Bohmont

Line drawings by Amanda L. Bohmont
Author photo by Rachelle Rios-LaRue

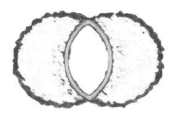

MANDORLA BOOKS
WWW.MANDORLABOOKS.COM

This collection of words is dedicated to my husband, Cory, and to my children, Jacob, Travis, Kyleigh, Ruby, Emmett and Phoebe—all of whom keep me grounded and surrounded in love and support.

TABLE OF CONTENTS

INTRODUCTION

Nothing can prepare you for grief. There really are no words that can adequately explain the intense sorrow of deep, heart-wrenching grief.

My beloved son, Emmett, transitioned while lying next to me in September 2018. To witness my child's last breath and see his soul leave his physical body catapulted me into the depths of despair. My son, my child, my baby had died and left me behind. Logic tells you that your children are not supposed to die before you. You are not supposed to bear witness to any kind of pain or suffering felt by your flesh and blood child, much less navigate hospitals and hospice. It feels completely out of balance when you plan a funeral for your precious baby.

Nonetheless, I found myself facing a horror that I didn't know existed. The agony of my loss was raw and consuming. I didn't know how to do grief. I don't think anybody does. Friends and family didn't seem to know what to say to me anymore, my husband became lost in his own grief, my other children were left shell-shocked and continued to look to me as mom and the one who had to have it all together. I was so confused by it all. I felt isolated and alone, bleeding and oh so empty. All while I was mourning my sweet baby boy, questioning his life and his death.

I was lost and frightfully sad. Days became increasingly dark as I struggled to find the light. I had become so blinded by the searing pain of missing my son that I grasped for anything to hold onto and anchor me. I needed space and a place to breathe. I desperately needed support but didn't seem to fit into typical grief groups. Psychologists, therapists, and church groups, who didn't experience loss of their own, didn't seem to understand my heartache and emptiness of having lost a child I once carried in my womb.

I started to turn within more and more, not finding support outside of myself. It was in the quiet expanse of within that I awakened to my Divine Light and Truth. It is where I remembered who I truly am, who my son is, and where he is. I connected with Emmett and with my authentic soul in ways I'd never learned how to before. And I knew. I just knew. I found the answers that I was seeking. I discovered my Divine Truth and recognized the innate Wisdom that flows through all of us.

I began to heal.

Grief is not permanent. Grief is a journey, a passage. If we allow it, grief is a voyage to the awakening of our soul and our Divine Truth and Love. It is a journey that might lead us to uncovering our soul's purpose.

Maybe we don't know what that purpose is at first, or maybe we think that little whisper in the back of our head is crazy and cannot be so. Yet, somehow, in saying "Yes" to it, we find ourselves doing something we never thought possible.

A couple of years after Emmett transitioned, I said "Yes" to my soul's purpose. Almost immediately, words began pouring through me. Words drenched in ancient wisdom and pure love. Words that would come fast and demand my full attention until I could get them out onto paper. It felt strange and yet more right and real than anything I have ever done before.

I would never have considered myself a writer or poet. I can't say that I have a degree in English or Literature. I'm just me. A woman, a wife, and a mother. I adore my husband and kids and love doing art and gardening and honeybees. I have a child that transitioned to the other side before me.

Yet, here I am.

Now, stepping over the threshold, I feel as if I'm standing in front of you naked and exposed. I've peeled back the layers of my human self, revealing my soul. My bright and beautiful, infinite soul. I feel so incredibly vulnerable and more alive than I ever have before.

I am Becoming.

In baring my soul to you, I have freed myself. Maybe that's the whole point of this life. The experiences we have and saying "Yes" to our soul's purpose can lead us on the journey to freedom. Real freedom. Not the kind that can be defined in the physical sense, but the kind that can only be felt and known within. It is in the surrender that true freedom is found.

I stand now, surrendered, free, and more powerful than I ever dreamed possible. It is in this surrender that I share these words with the world. I know these words come from a higher source, the Divine Source, the Source of Knowing that dwells within each of us. These poems are not mine to keep tucked away, safe from scrutiny. They are for others. They must be shared and felt and experienced. I offer them to you with outstretched arms and open hands.

May you be gentle and savor them the way that I do. May they awaken your soul and rekindle a spark long forgotten within you. May you be reminded of your truth and your beautiful light. May you feel yourself held in love and peace. May you remember that healing is possible.

I am wrapping you, Dear One, in infinite love and light.

Amanda

Becoming

THE BECOMING

It is not the same for everyone.
Sometimes it happens all at once.
Much of the time it happens slowly, over time.
Never something you intended or thought would happen
    to you.

You can't force it.
Most often you resist it.
Or doubt it, or think you're not worthy.
But once you begin, there's no stopping the Becoming.
And you are no longer the same person.

What sets the Becoming in motion is different for every
    person.
Maybe it was a shattering of deep grief and pain of loss.
Maybe it was a horrific, unimaginable trauma.
Maybe you don't even know the exact moment or event.
Whatever the cause, there is no going back,

Only forward.

There is no going back to your old self.
Your old ways.
Your old habits.

Nothing will taste the same, sound the same or feel the
   same.
Everything will look different and even smell different.
It's bizarre. And unexplainable.
And no matter how hard you might try, it is impossible
   to return to the before.

So you let it happen.

You Become.

After the initial resistance, you begin to settle into the
   process.
And eventually you realize that you are Becoming more
   you than you've ever been before.
Your heart fractures wide open and you remember who
   you are.
You Become Light and Love and all things Big and
   Beautiful and True.
You Become raw and authentic, gentler and more
   compassionate.
You have a new found understanding and tolerance.
You hear clearly your innate knowledge and wisdom.
And you begin to recognize that there was no other way
   for you than this.

The Becoming is sacred work.
Holy work.
Pure work.
Quiet work.

You allow the Love and the Knowing to flow through
   you.
You Become whole and complete.

You honor the Light inside of you,
You honor the Light you now see in every other, living
   thing
And you are overwhelmed with the deepest of gratitude.

You Become still.
You Become aware of the Divine peace and Love within
   you.

You release yourself to Grace and heal.

You are transformed.

You have Become.

TO LISTEN

We become still.
We empty ourselves
of all thoughts, all pretenses, all judgment
and just be.
Only then are we ready and able to invite another to
    open themselves to us
so that we may listen.

We lean in, and we pay attention to,
not only their words,
but their actions,
their nuances,
their tone of voice,
their facial expressions,
their fidgets.

We listen not only with our ears
but with our minds,
our hearts,
our souls.
We listen with our entire being.

We hold the space
for as long as,
as much as

is needed.

We hear what lies beneath the words.
We hear what is not being said out loud.

Most oftentimes that is enough.
To listen.
Because everyone carries within them their truth.
They already know.
They just needed to be heard.
They just needed another
to hold the space.
And be willing to listen.

Listening is one of the greatest gifts we can give another
It is a selfless gift.
It is a gift of pure love
and Divine Grace.
Oh! How beautiful and magnificent it is to give a gift
    such as this.

After a time, you begin to realize that you, in fact, are
    not the only giver.
You are, in fact, the receiver of a precious gift yourself.
You have been given the gift of seeing inside another's
    most vulnerable self.
You were the chosen one to hear the heartache and
    angst, the joys and sorrows, deepest fears and
    triumphs, secret loves and longings.
You get a glimpse inside another's soul at their beautiful
    light.

You are deeply grateful and forever humbled
that you were trusted to be the one to see them so bare.
How precious indeed is it to see another in this way.

Bare.

If only we saw every other this way.
If only the world saw us this way.

Bare
and breathtakingly beautiful.

We have the ability to give this gift to everyone.
It is so simple really.
All that must be done is
to become still
and to listen.

TO BEGIN AGAIN

It will take every fiber of your being
to muster the courage to take another step.

To carry on.

To begin again.

Dear One.
I know the strength it will take.
I know the fortitude that you must muster.
I know the fear you grasp onto so tightly.
I know the despair that has become your identity.

I see you.

Lean in on me,
I will lend you my strength,
for as long as you need
for as far as you need until you feel steady enough on
    your own.

I implore you.
I beg you.
I encourage you.

It is okay
to begin again.
You have permission.

Close your eyes.
Take a deep breath.
Just begin.

You will not regret it.
You might fall down,
you will stumble along the way.
But you can do this.
Take the first step.

Take that first trembling step forward.
Unsure of your grounding,
unsure of the unknown.

The frightening unknown.

I know what it is to be so timid, doubtful, hesitant
too scared to come out of your comfort,
blinded by the darkness that surrounds,
questioning everything you thought you knew.

I see you.

And I say to you
don't let the fear hold you back.

Back from discovering something even greater than you
    can possibly imagine.
Back from knowing your light.
Your truth.
Your purpose.
Your calling.

Lean in on me,
I will lend you my strength.
We will take the step together.

And I will forever remind you,
as a whisper in your heart,
I see you, Dear One.
You can do this,
you must do this.

Take the step and begin.

Begin again.

And again
and again if necessary.

For as long as it takes.

OUR TEARS

Cry, Dear One.
Let your tears flow freely.
Allow them to stain your face.
Do not be ashamed.
Don't try to hide them.

Cry, for as long as you need
as often as you'd like.
Cry for the joyous love, the lost love.
Cry for the heartache and loss,
for the longing and despair.
Cry for the exuberating happiness and the intense, sharp
   pain.
Cry for that which tugs on your heart and the could-
   have-beens.
Cry for the beauty of Grace, the beauty of Divine's
   creation.
Cry through the laughter and through the suffering.
Cry for the endings and the new beginnings.
Cry through your deepest grief and your greatest
   triumphs.

Cry, Dear One.

Tears are a testament of your courage, your grit, your
    tenacity.
They are not a sign of weakness.
No,
they are a sign of your strength.
Do not hold them back.

Tears are not forever.
This is not who you are.
They are a reminder of the deep, deep love within you.

Allow the release and the flow of emotion to come up
    and out of you.
Tears can cleanse our hearts,
and our souls.
They are the messengers of our great joys, deepest
    sorrows and our truth.
They help teach us who we are.
Tears are precious indeed.

Ugly, hard, or gentle tears.
It matters not.
You are beautiful still.
Your light shines so brightly.
I see you.

Cry, Dear One.
Let it out.

Allow me to collect your sacred tears,
your sacred memories,
your sacred love and pain.
I will hold them close.
If ever you forget your strength
I will show you your holy tears,
and remind you always of the deep unending Love and
    Truth of who you are.

OUR FEELINGS

Our happiness, sadness, love and heartache,
Our anger and frustration, joy and bliss,
They are all teachers.
Invite them to come, listen to what they have to whisper.
You can learn the truth about yourself.
You can learn from what is felt deep inside.
Lean into what memories come up,
what triggers might have set you off,
what makes you sad and, oh, so joyous.
Like all teachers, they come and go, each time with a
    different lesson.
Embrace the lesson.
Embrace the feeling,
and know that you are that much stronger and more
    authentically you for having felt that.

Feelings can come destructive and all consuming, they
    can knock you off your feet and envelop you with
    no escape, as if they are trying to break you.
Feelings can come as a soft blanket of warmth and
    comfort making you feel so full of love and security,
    as if you might burst open.
Allow it.
Allow all of this.
Allow yourself to feel them deeply,
allow your feelings to surface,

but don't let them linger.
Don't allow them to get comfortable and stay
   indefinitely.

Lean in, listen, learn. And release.

Once a feeling has done its work, it is time to let go of
   that feeling.
Blow it away, gently, as if it's nestled on a dandelion
   seed.
Permit the winds of the universe to sweep it up and
   away.
Watch as it floats up to the heavens.
Give humbled gratitude for the lesson it brought,
for the space it created
and for the Love and Light and Truth it left behind.

Negative emotions desire to take up room, don't allow
   them.
Positive emotions often never seem to stay long, leaving
   all too soon.
Feelings can be hard and painful. They can be confusing
   and difficult to understand.
It can seem as if your feelings are a never ending
   rollercoaster with ups and downs and twists and
   turns, spiraling you out of control.
All of that is okay.
It is normal and what makes us human.

Breathe,
take a breath.

Know that you are so much more than your feelings.
Your feelings do not define who you are
they are not forever.
Don't wrap your identity around a feeling.
That is not you, not your Truth.
You are Divine Love and Light, full of Knowing and
    Wisdom.
You are so beautiful, no matter how you might feel.

Feel.
Feel all of it.
Don't be afraid to feel.

You are not your feelings, Dear One.
You are so much more.
I see you so clearly,
So purely,
so brightly shining your Divine Light.

BELIEVE

Believe in yourself.
You are so much more than what you see on the surface.
You are stronger
more powerful than you can imagine.
Believe in your inner Light and the inner Light within
    others.
Believe in those gut feelings of intuition
and knowing.

Believe in God, Source, the Divine, the Universe.
As this is you.
You are a Divine expression of God created in pure
    Love and Light.

Believe in all things big and beautiful and true.
Believe in love and joy.
Believe in the miracle and perfection of creation,
of all creation,
and the One who created it.

Believe in angels and fairies,
beings from other planets.
Believe in the multiverses and timelessness.
Believe in the immeasurable cosmos.
Look up and know there is vastly more than here.

Lift your face to the heavens, close your eyes, extend
    your arms and feel yourself part of something
    infinitely bigger than this moment.

Believe in the Truth of Wholeness and Oneness.

Believe in all that is kept hidden away inside of your
    heart.
Open your heart, allow it all to come up and out.
Ground yourself in understanding of who you truly are,
an eternal soul of Love and Light created by God, for
    God, as God.

Believe in the possibility of more.
Believe in your Truth.
Believe in Divine design.
It is no accident that you are here,
now,
in this specific physical form.
Believe in your purpose.

Believe, Dear One.
Believe in all that you can not see or touch
feel them, instead, with your heart and soul.
Go within.
Feel and know.
Extend outward
shining your Love and Light.

And always Believe.

THE SHATTERING

Not ever something you planned for,
or imagined could possibly happen to you.

Not ever something you can prepare for,
or imagined you would be forced to endure.

One moment, life is as you know it.
The next,
you are catapulted into the depths of despair.
An abyss of suffering,
deep,
dark,
and, oh, so excruciating.

At first you are dazed and confused by the unexpected
    pain,
the searing pain of instantaneous grief and loss.
A pain so great you feel as if you have broken into a
    bazillion pieces.

You find yourself hurting so bad you begin to scream
    and flail looking for relief.
You have no idea if others heard the scream so deep
    inside of you.
Your brain can't comprehend,

can't understand,
and refuses to acknowledge
the loss.

Your breath shortens.
Oftentimes you don't even realize you're holding it
until your lungs burn so bad you have to let it out.
And when it comes out,
it comes as a wail.
A deep, primitive, carnal wail
of despair,
of agony,
of sorrow.

You can't hear anything around you.
You're unaware of those surrounding you.
You're blinded by the tears and anguish.
Your body starts shaking uncontrollably.
Your hands start grasping the air
searching for anything to hold onto
and anchor you
so that you are not completely swept away with the
    sudden wave of grief.

Your heart beats faster and harder.
As if it might explode from your chest.
It pounds in your ears,
reminding you,
taunting you,
proving to you how you are still alive.

And all you think is "Take me too."

Take. Me. Too.

Loved ones reach out to touch and comfort you,
to help pull you up off the floor,
to quiet your hacking sobs.

But there is nothing that can reach you now
to soften the blow.
It is too dark, too severe, too painful.
You feel completely ripped apart.
Left bleeding and drowning. Deeper and deeper into a
    sea of sadness.

Nobody knows this gaping wound.
Nobody truly understands.
It is not for others to know or carry.

Only you.

Only you feel this pain so raw and throbbing.
Only you feel the enormous hole and emptiness.
Only you know the love and now the intense loss.

You find yourself suspended in a void of time.
The only time that matters are the moments before.
You long to go back in time for one more breath,
one more moment,
one more touch.

There are no stitches or salves for this kind of wound.
This pain is not the way of the world as we know it.
How can a human possibly hurt so bad?

When all emotion,
all fear,
anger,
despair,
longing,
is spent out of you,
you become numb.
And you welcome the numbness as a relief to the
excruciating pain you feel burning within.

Your heart still pounds in your ears,
your tears still stain your face,
your brain still begs, "Take me too."
You see only darkness now.

Then you realize, you are no longer the you from a
breath ago.

That you has been completely and utterly

Shattered.

TAKE FLIGHT

Trepid, at first,
excited for the possibility,
anxious for the unknown.
Step out.
Spread your wings.

Take flight.
Let your soul soar.

Burst forward,
take to the skies.
Do not waiver.
Do not doubt.
Never apologize.

Solidly grounded only in your knowing,
trust your internal navigation
to guide you always.

And fly.

Spiral outward and upward.
It does not matter the destination,
all is awaiting your arrival.
Listen to the voice within.

Let the winds of the universe carry you up and away.
Let the sun reflect off your wings signaling your flight.

Soar.

Don't be scared
take a deep breath.
Graceful,
sure
and true.

Savor the adventure.
Bask in the freedom.
Intentional,
guided
and courageous.

Take flight.
Let your soul soar.

And fly away home.

STOP RESISTING

Stop resisting
Let go
Let go of your ideals of how this life should look
Let go of your ideals of how people should act
Let go
Let go of all of the preconceptions
They are not true
They are not you
Stop resisting the change that's happening within
Don't fight it
I know that it's uncomfortable
I know how confusing it seems
Up is down and down is up
Allow it
Allow yourself to break open
To step into the unknown
Stop resisting
Allow yourself to be free
Free
Be free and discover your purpose.
Become who you are meant to be
I promise you, Dear One
You will not regret it
You will soar
Stop resisting

Allow the process

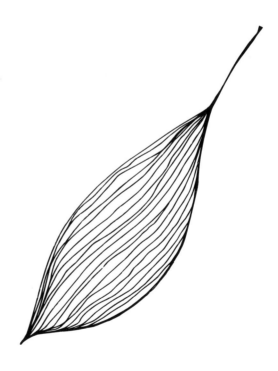

TIME

What if time did not exist?
What would you choose to do?
Work, play, rest, create?

What if the only thing that governed your day was the
sun and moon?
And not a clock?
How many hours would you spend with family and
friends?
Or alone in silent meditation?

What if time is only an illusion?
The clock face a lie intended to trap you in a daily grind
meant to disorient you and trick you into believing
in something finite?
What would you change as you awakened to this truth?

THE CHOICE

In every situation.
In every encounter.
In every moment.
You have a choice.

What you choose may lead you down a path of more
    obstacles.
Maybe a path of great turmoil.
Maybe your choice leaves you stagnant and stuck.
Or maybe your choice sets you free.
And this one freeing choice leads to another and then
    another.

All choices made are opportunities to learn and to grow.
All choices made are teachers that can help guide.
All choices made create space for your soul to expand
    and for you to discover your truth.

Don't play victim and say you have no choice.
That is an excuse, a cop-out.
This is a lie that you are telling yourself.
There is always a choice.
Always.

Maybe the choice is large or small.

Maybe others notice what you choose.
Maybe only your heart knows the choice.
It matters not.

Choose to stand bravely in your truth.
Choose to listen to your soul.
Choose to live fully and unabashedly.
Choose to heal.
Choose to love.
Choose to shine your light.

There is no one else responsible for your choices but
     you.
You hold the power to choose for yourself.
Don't put blame on others.
Don't give away your power.

You were Divinely created and given the gift of choice.
Use your gift.

You can choose to live in love and not fear.
You can choose to be gentle and kind.
You can choose to go within to know your Truth and
     feel at peace.
You have the ability,
you just have to make the choice.

I see you, Dear One.
Standing at your crossroads,
newly aware of the Divine gift of choice.

I know the strength it will take.

It is a brave thing to choose.

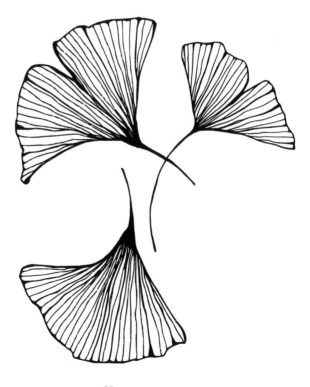

THE FLAME

Imagine a flame.
A warm flame. Flickering, soft and gentle.
Imagine that flame filling your home with light.
And with love.

Now imagine that home as your heart.
This flame glowing inside of you, filling you with light
    and love and warmth.
Never fading, never going out.
Flickering, burning, illuminating always.
Feel the comfort, the love and the gentleness.
Embrace this flame with gratitude for filling your home
    with light.

Now imagine this flame that fills your home that is your
    heart with light,
warm, soft and gentle,
flickering inside each and every being.
Imagine each other's flame within.
Look beyond the exterior of the physical body,
allow the personality to fall away,
see only the flickering light of love and warmth that is
    within.

Know that the flame that is light that is within you,

is the same flame in others.
Flickering, burning, illuminating always.
Embrace the flame,
embrace all others
with sincere gratitude,
knowing we are all the same Divine Light.

BALANCE

There is magic and wisdom
to be found in nature.
If we choose to notice it.

It is when we slow down
to do the noticing,
when we immerse ourselves
into the natural world,
that we awaken to the small miracles of nature's
wonders.

We begin to feel
and understand
and hear
and recognize
the rhythm
of all creation.

We become aware of
how we are actually
no greater than,
no less than,

but the same as,

the busiest of honeybee
or graceful deer
or intelligent dolphin.

We all have a place,
as the same,
in perfect balance and harmony with all.

I AM

I am word.
I am the sun and moon, planet and stars.
I am every person that has ever walked or will walk this
     earth.
I am every bird that flies in the sky,
every fish that swims in the sea.
I am every breath you take,
every giggle and tear you shed.
I am every snowflake falling and flower blooming.
I am every hidden insect and tiny piece of ocean algae.
I am every whisper of love,
every act of compassion.
I am every moment of joy and present even in the
     moments of terror.
I am every pure thought,
every kind word spoken.
I am every brush stroke of art and lyric in songs,
every sweet melody of music playing.
I am the fog rolling through the valleys.
I am the forest and mountain and plains,
every river and lake and ocean.
I am every leaf that buds,
every grain of sand at the beach.
I am the wind, the rain,
every rainbow and cloud in the sky.

I am the flame flickering within you.
I am all living things.
I am everywhere.
I am everything.
I Am.

RISE

The time is coming near.
Get ready to rise.
Get ready to rise up and become who you came here to
    become.
Arise from the dust,
from the ashes,
from the mud.
Get ready to rise.

YOUR NAME

What is a name?
A name?
A name?

Is it just arbitrary letters and sounds, placed together?
Consonants and vowels creating syllables, creating
    tempo?

How was it chosen?
And why?
Weeded out from a list? Passed down from generations?
It was no accident you were named what you were, Dear
    One.
Whispers from the universe, nudges from the angels
all helped land your name upon you in this lifetime.
Have you lived many lifetimes with a name similar?

Does your name tell a story?
Is it steeped in history, rich in origin and meaning?
Stories of old,
stories yet to unfold.

Do you allow your name to define you?
Do you allow your name to hold you back?
Is it heavy with the weight of expectation?

Or is it freeing?
Creating space to rise to the vibration of your name?

Embrace your chosen name.
Define for yourself what it means,
by your actions, your words, your deeds.
Define for yourself what your name embodies.
Define for yourself by breathing your purpose, your
    calling into the nature of your name.

What is a name?
A name?
A name?

Does your essence, your spirit, your soul have a name?
A name given to you when Divine Creator breathed life
    into your being.
What is that name?
What are the sounds, the tones, the colors?
This name carries on for eternity.
It carries your truth, for forever, into every lifetime and
    beyond.

Say it in your heart.
Say it again.
I can hear you, Dear One
I can hear your true authentic name,
drenched in love and meaning.

Learn your name.

Hear your name.
Speak your name.
Know your name.

What is your name?
Your name?
Your name?

SAY YES

Say yes to the transformation.
Say yes to the expansion.
To the remembering of the truth within you.

Say yes to shedding of the old.
Let go of the old ideals,
old constructs
old self.

Say yes to the dawning of the new.
The new awareness,
new beginnings
new authentic self.

Let go of the fear.
Release your grasp on your current beliefs,
they no longer serve you.

Open yourself to receiving.
Be ready for the work ahead,
for the journey at hand.

Say yes to the lessons,
the resurrection,
the mission.
Say yes.

BE

Be.
Be where you are.
Right here,
right now.
Don't worry how you look,
or where you're at,
what you might be missing,
or what obligations you might have.
Allow the world to stop spinning for just a moment.

Be.
Be here.
In the now.
In the present.
Be still.
Be quiet.

Take a breath.
Close your eyes.
Take another breath,
deep and full,
expanding your lungs
filling every crevasse within your body with life force.

Hold it a moment.

Do you feel the peace and calm?
Can you remember your Wholeness and Light?
Do you hear your spirit whispering your Divine Truth?

Now, let go of your breath.
Releasing, slowly, steady, what is no longer serving you.
Empty yourself fully.

And be.
Just for a moment
before the world starts spinning again.
Be still.
Be here.
Be now.
Just be.

THE LIGHTHOUSE

You are a lighthouse.
Beckoning others to safety.
Your inner light shines as that guidepost.
Ushering others into remembering their own light.
So many are lost in the dark.

But you.
You, Dear One,

are standing rooted and firm amongst the darkness.
Surrounded by the night sky of turmoil and angst and
    grief.
Shining your light,
brightly
unwavering
for as far as anyone can see
heralding to those looking
reminding others of their own strength and ability to
    come home.

Home to safe harbor.

There can be no darkness when your light is shining.
Occasionally it may dim as the fog of more grief rolls in.
But never will it be extinguished.

Your light is clear and sure and strong and true.
Always there.

Anchored solidly, steady and steadfast in Divine Truth
and Love.

SURRENDER

Surrender yourself.

Surrender all parts of your being.
Your mind and thoughts,
your ego,
feelings,
even, your body as actions.

Surrender.

Surrender it all to Divine Grace and Knowing.
Surrender it all to your higher self and angel guides.
Listen to the voice heard deep within.
Discern your truth.

Savor the peace found inside when you're completely
    surrendered.
Lean into the wholeness.

And be free.

ONENESS

All of Creation,

the oceans and rivers, lakes and ponds,
lush forests of trees and plants,
every creature that roams on land,
swims in the sea
and soars in the air,

All understand Oneness.

These living things don't know the difference of
anything other than One.

They know that
Oneness is your true state of being.
It is the truth about you,
but many have forgotten.

Let me help remind you, Dear One.

You are One.
We are One.
One with All of Creation.
And as we know God expresses God by creating All of
nature,

and souls and stars and colors and tones of sounds,
and as we know we are One with nature,
we know we are One with God.

We are as God.
As One.
One heartbeat.
One flame.
One Consciousness.

Imagine the beach, Dear One,
covered in tiny specks of sand,
being moved by the powerful ocean waves.
Pushed out to sea,
washed upon the shore,
blanketing the ocean floor.
Sand as One.

Many particles, specks, pieces, but still One sand.
You can scoop up a bucket of sand,
or a handful of sand,
it is still sand.
It is still part of the sandy beach.
It is still One with itself.

You can build great sandcastles,
or track it on your feet all the way home,
and it remains sand.
Part of One sand.

You can dump your buckets back into the ocean and the
    sand combines once again with the sandy shore as
    One.
You will never find the end of the grains of sand.
Nor could you ever find the beginning of the sandy
    shore.

All is One.
No beginning.
No ending.
All as God's Creation and Delight and Love.
As One.

You are that grain of sand, Dear One.
We are that sand.
Possibly separate from the others,
but forever part of the whole,
the collective.
As one.

We are One consciousness,
and just as there are many,
too many to count, grains of sand,
So too are there stars in the multiverses.
So too are there pure souls of Divine Light.
So too is the Love that is the Creator
That is in you
That is you
Connecting us All
as One.

YOU DO NOT HAVE TO BE GOOD

You do not have to be good at something.
You simply have to do it.
Over and over and over again.
Don't let perfection hold you back.
Get up and do.

Put your phone down and return to the time where there
    was no social media for distraction,
no selfies for instant gratification, no electronic games
    for stimulation.
Go back to a simpler time, a slower pace.
And remember the joy and relaxation found in creating.
And in doing something that moves your soul.

Keep your hands and fingers and bodies engaged.
It helps the mind slow down and listen.
It is in the listening that you discover your truth.
It is in the listening that you hear the soft whispers of
    inspiration.

Create. Do. Flow. Move.
Something. Anything.
Over and over and over again.

You do not have to be good.
You just have to do.

FEARLESS

Be fearless and don't hold back.
Don't second guess yourself.
Charge forward with resolute courage.
Knowing the power of your Divine Truth surrounds and
    envelops you in protective white light.
Like a shield of steel armor plate.

You can do anything, Dear One.
You have permission to be fearless.

Step fearlessly into your purpose.
Take one.
Then two.
Soon a dozen
steps into your destiny,
and beyond.

COCOONED

Sometimes the world feels as if it's too much,
as if everything is coming at you and overtaking you,
like you just need to hide and retreat from it all.

Cocoon yourself, Dear One.
Wrap yourself tight so that you feel sheltered and held,
safe and secure.
Nestled in quiet refuge.

Take all the time you need here.
Feel all the feels,
the uncertainty, the questions, the sadness.
Allow it to wash over and through you.

And when you are ready,
when you have fully ruptured,
when the darkness and pain have been transmuted,
when you are through putting back the pieces,
emerge again.

Brilliant and dazzling.

For it is from within those cracks that your light shines
    forth.
A testament of your strength and love.

NONJUDGMENT

There is a shedding process,
if we allow,
that happens, naturally, over time.

Trees shed their leaves when the leaves no longer
provide nutrients.
Animals shed their fur when the fur no longer is needed
to keep them warm.
Humans shed their skin as new skin cells are created and
replaced.

So too, we, as souls, as embodiment of Divine Love and
Light,
So too, we, as souls, shed our old ways when those old
ways no longer serve us.
We shed our thoughts, our ideals, our concepts, our
constructs, our perceptions, even our patterns when
they no longer align with the truth of who we are.
And as this natural process occurs, our judgments fall
away too,
just as the leaves, the fur, the skin.

As we awaken to our true selves,
and remember that our human ego is just a perception, a
hologram, an untruth,
our judgments are shed as they no longer serve our ego.

We notice ourselves not judging others, but also notice that we are no longer aware or concerned with how others may judge us.

The worry and fear of not fitting in, not having enough, not looking or acting or being a certain way is simply no longer there.

And we find ourselves in place of being, existing, in a higher frequency, where opinions and judgments do not dwell.

We find ourselves in a place of peace and serenity and pure joy.

We find ourselves in a place of nonjudgment.

We discover our authentic self and thrive in ways that we didn't even know were possible.

We are free.

Free to become who we were created to be.

Free to let our souls soar.

Free to reside in Divine Light and Truth, connected to All.

Whole.

And as One.

MOTHERS

To all the mommas, the women, the mothers, the moms,
To the ones who carried their sons and daughters in
their womb, felt their baby move, heard the
heartbeat of life within and bravely birthed their
child,
The ones who selflessly gave their hearts to a child not
of their womb, who opened themselves to the
young ones seeking a mothers love and warm home,
To the ones who've suffered a miscarriage, anticipating
life and possibility one moment, and facing intense
loss and confusion the next,
The ones who felt battled with the decision to abort an
unwanted pregnancy, feeling as if they had no
choice other than this,
To the ones who have been through the rollercoaster of
shots of hormones, the insane cost and intrusiveness
of IVF only to have their hopes come crashing
down or greatest dream realized,
To the ones who've suffered the shattering of the
passing of their child, who with chin quivering, eyes
to heaven carries on and mothers their child on the
other side,
The ones who are called auntie, grandma, sister or
teacher, even the ones who nurture and care for an
animal or pet, or elderly parent, or career, you are a
mother, of sorts too,

To the ones who mother one, two or ten beautiful souls,
   who nourish, nurture, who love, who hold their
   breath as they watch their baby take a first step,
   learn to ride a bike, drive away in a car, get married,
   and one day have a child of their own,

I see you, Dear One.

I see your courage, tenacity and strength.
Your love, kindness and concern.
I see your deep wrinkles that were etched with
   compassion.
Your gray hairs grown out of fret and innate wisdom.
I hear you laugh deeply and worry just as hard.
I hold sacred your tears of joy and tears of sorrow.
I feel your pride and disappointment.
I realize the anxiety and strong will.
I understand the sacrifices you've made.
I smile at your dreams, your wishes, your deepest heart's
   desires
for yourself, as well as those dreams you hold for your
   young.

To become a mother, to watch your heart walk outside
   of your body, to say yes to the hardest role on the
   planet,
to nurture another soul, another being,
to serve another human,
is to answer one of the greatest and noblest of callings.

I humbly thank you, and give gratitude for your
    perseverance.

It doesn't matter how good or how bad or what kind of
    mom you are,
it doesn't matter your mistakes, regretful decisions, your
    imperfections.
It doesn't matter.

You are perfect.

You were chosen to mother your child exactly how
    you're doing it.
It is all Divine planning,
Full of great love and intention for your personal growth
    and expansion.

I see your Light, Beautiful One,
I see your Love and Grace,
your sacrifice and juggling of schedules and budgets.
I know what you have given up to be where you are
    now,
your body and comfort, time and energy.
You have allowed your old identity and ideals to fall
    away.
All for another.

To mother a child is both the hardest and most
    rewarding thing we can do.
It is a selfless gift that we give to another.

It is in the giving that we discover the Truth of who we
are.
It is the true essence of yourself as a Divine soul of Love
and Light.

I see you Dear One,
And I honor the work that you are doing.
The lessons you are learning.
The heart that you witness, as your baby, navigating this
big wide world.

I say thank you.
And I so deeply praise and adore you.

POSSIBILITY

All things are possible when you go within to your
reservoir of knowledge and wisdom
and remember your truth.

You are limitless.

There are no rules,
no constraints.
Do not be fooled,
for it was external forces
that has limited you.

You can do anything.

Feel yourself free as you float in your ocean of
possibility.

Everything,
everything is inside of you.

Let it flow through you,
and out of you.

Pick up the paint brush, the pen.
Pick up the chisel, the hammer, the garden hoe.

Pick up your tablet, the 3 inch thick book.
What is your deepest dream and desire?

Bathe yourself.
Immerse yourself.
Drench yourself in your pool of wisdom.
Return to the waters of knowledge,
creativity and truth.

Know the possibility that is you,

as the created
and the creator.

THE SNOW

Glistening like hundreds of millions of tiny diamonds,
Like magical fairy dust thrown from the heavens,
falling softly, gently before settling upon the earth.
Draping itself over every tree branch, every rock and
  crevasse on the ground.
A duvet covering the landscape in purity and renewal.
Forcing all of nature and its inhabitants to rest.
To snuggle down even deeper,
to become still and quiet.

The sunlight twinkles off the droplets of ice and snow.
Shimmery, glittery,
reflecting the truth of what is within all of us-
Light,
Hope,
Serenity.

The tree's branches bow in majesty under the weight of
  the blanket laid.
The blue sky sings in exaltation of the Creator's glory.
The sun warms the earth bringing those resting to life
  once again.
Leaves rustle ever so gently in the wind.
Squirrels and birds scamper easily across the white quilt
  of snow.

Sounds are muffled.
Only the sounds of your own heartbeat can be heard
as you watch your breath exhale into the air.
Life force billowing outward from your physical body.
Reminding you of the now, this one breath, this one
    moment.

You can hear the whispers of the universe in the stirring
    of the snow covered topography.
You can see the light of your truth glimmer across the
    landscape.
You can feel the peace that has enveloped the earth and
    your heart.

SEA OF GRIEF

Tears of longing for the one you've lost.
Tears of hopelessness and despair.
Angry tears.
Confused tears.
Heartbroken tears.
Tears of emptiness.
Gallons and gallons and gallons of tears.
An ocean created by your salty tears.
Your own personal sea of grief.

Vast.
Seemingly unending.
Stretching for miles and miles in all directions.
Violent waters.
Menacing clouds.
Making it hard to tell where the sky ends and ocean
    begins.
All melding together
as one dark angry salty empty space that becomes your
    new reality.

Treading water is impossible.
There are no lifelines.
No buoys.
Nothing to save you.

Flailing and grasping for anything to hold onto and keep
    your head above water,
exhausted by the effort,
you allow yourself to slip beneath the water's surface.
Floating.
Unmoving.
Suspended.
Lungs burning.
Releasing yourself to the pain.
Accepting your fate.

And then you kick.
Once,
twice.
Your head breaks through the water.
You gasp for another breath,
coughing and sputtering
just as a massive wave crashes overhead and forces you
    beneath the surface again.
Over and over and over again, this repeats.

And then one day,
as your head breaks the surface,
the wave doesn't crash on top of you.
You take a moment a float,
breathing,
face upturned to the heavens.

More time passes.
Less effort to float.

Fewer waves come crashing down.
You learn to tread water.

The sun peeks through the clouds and warms your face.
You don't feel like you might drown anymore.
Eventually, you notice a lifeboat.
Wondering if it has always been there.

In time, you find your way to shore.

At any moment, you might become lost in your sea of
    grief again.
Being taken under
waves crashing hard overhead.

But this time,
you remember,
that the seas do calm,
that there is a lifeboat waiting.

You can find the shore again.

One day, you leave the shore
and discover that life has continued.
You hesitantly join in.
You're different though, forever changed.
You accept that you have not moved on from your grief,
you simply have learned how to carry on.

You can always return to your sea of grief.

It is yours.
No one else's.

At some point, though, as you stand on the shore,
looking out across your sea of grief,
you don't see the threatening, angry ocean.
You are not scared of the waters.

You only see the tears and tears and gallons of tears

of love.

And realize,

grief is but love.

WE ARE THE SAME

Regardless of anything.
Anything.
Our skin color,
where we are from, our upbringing,
our careers, our genders or partners,
our societal judgments of goodness,
our life's journey,
our own remembering,

We are the same.

The same light.
The same flame.
The same Divine Truth.
We were created in the same Love.

We are the same gust of wind.
The same strong and sturdy tree,
reaching to the heavens,
stretching its roots deep into the earth.

We are the same grain of sand.
And rolling wave,
blade of grass,
and unique snowflake.

We are the same mountain top and wide river
bubbling, flowing, meandering with the terrain.
We are the same blossoming flower
and gentle honeybee upon it.

We are the same laugh.
The same twinkle in an eye,
tear rolling down a cheek.
We are the same breath.
The same heartbeat.

We are the same beating of one heart.
As we dance to the same song.
As we vibrate to the same symphony.
As we burst forth in color and sound, harmoniously,
    vibrantly, each one necessary to complete the
    masterpiece.

We are all connected.
All One.

We are the same One.

Feel the Oneness.
The sameness.

Feel all of the stars and stars and stars.
Multiverses of stars.
Feel it with your truth.
Lean into the feeling.

Know the rhythmic heartbeat
of all of the souls and souls and souls.
Beautiful,
perfect,
souls of light,
and of love.

We are the same.
The same.
The same.

OUR PARTNERSHIPS

I hear wise words of self understanding and higher
    consciousness.
I read thoughts on passionate lovers and soul mates,
    twin flames.
But where are the words and thoughts of a partner?
A life partner,
a spouse, a mate or companion?
Where is the 'how to' of a marriage or partnership while
    journeying on the path of spiritual awakening?

All of the great gurus, teachers, and wise ones,
where are their partners?
And why didn't they talk to the everyday love and
    commitment, passion and companionship of their
    partners, the disagreements, and let downs, the
    hurtful words and fights?

Being with another, coexisting, partnering can be
    confusing,
and lonely at times,
and can seem overwhelming.
Two divine souls, two human egos and personalities
meshing, combining, overlapping space with their own
    likes and dislikes, schedules and ideals.
Where are the wise words on how to make these things
    work?

What does a marriage even mean?

How is it supposed to look?

How do we maintain an authentic version of ourselves
while sharing parts of ourselves with our partners?

So much of our life journey is spent learning personal
lessons, growing and evolving into higher frequency
and consciousness, remembering our wholeness and
our Oneness and our divine soul and grace of the
truth of who we are.

But as we go through this self-discovery,

What of our partners?

And how do they fit into our Oneness?

How do we navigate a life with another when that other
doesn't remember what we've remembered?

When that other no longer sees eye to eye with you?

No longer has the same dreams and ideals as you?

What then?

We stand in our frequency of love.

We stand in our wholeness and Oneness.

We stand in our knowing,

and in our choosing of our life with our partner.

We shine even brighter than we ever have before.

We use words of love and understanding and
compassion and empathy.

We fiercely respect, first ourselves and then our partners.

We release and let go of our societal ideals of marriages
and companionship.

We release and let go of our desire to control our
    partners actions and reactions, words and decisions.
We release and let go of our partners.

And embrace, instead, with our hearts our authentic self.
We embrace with our arms our beloved partners.
We see them as beautiful authentic souls, too.

We remember our truth,

Our Divine Truth.

Maybe our partner of today is not the same as of next
    month or year or ten years.
Maybe our partner is the exact same person from our
    teenagehood through adulthood and the one
    holding our hand when we transition to the other
    side.
It is not for us to know, or even understand.
It is for us to honor and respect and find the lesson and
    embrace the growth that occurs.
For every person that comes into our life comes to help
    serve us in learning a lesson,
help serve us in bringing us closer to ourselves.

Love.

True and pure love,
first for yourself, then for another.
It is when you know your Oneness and love yourself
    deeply that you are able to release the need for

another's love or affirmation or acceptance.
You release the need
for anything.

The best, longest lasting, truest partnerships
are the ones where you can stand alone.
Side by side.
Not entwined.
Not leaning on one another.
Not completing each other.
But solid, strong, steadfast in each of your truths.
Side by side.
Each whole.
Each One.
Each your own beautiful flame of light.
Burning, shining,
glowing for all to see.
Side by side.
As One.

TO FORGIVE

It's not easy at first,
to forgive.
It's not something that comes as second nature to most.

People may question or wonder why and how.
Some may refuse.
Some may forgive in words only,
keeping their hearts hardened and unmoving.

Lean in, Dear One.
Let me remind you of your Truth.

The one that must be forgiven first, is You.
Once you forgive yourself,
forgiving another simply happens.

Forgive yourself for not knowing,
for acting as your human ego and personality.
Forgive yourself for those hateful or cruel thoughts you
    have,
for withholding love, for yourself and others.
Forgive yourself for being blinded by the bitterness,
for the darkness that may have crept in.
Forgive yourself for the mistakes you've made,
for the choices you wish you could take back.

Forgive yourself for the words and actions that you
regret now.

We are all doing the best we can.
We have all forgotten our truth.
It is You that matters.
Only You.
Give yourself permission.
Show yourself grace and love.
Become still and quiet.
Whisper in your heart "I forgive myself. I forgive myself.
I forgive myself."

It is in the forgiving of yourself that will have the biggest
impact.
It will have a lasting and profound affect in your own life
and the life of all of those around you.
For when you do this,
when you forgive yourself,
a weight is lifted.
You are free.

And you find yourself residing in a place where
forgiveness is your true nature.
Because you see and know others for who they truly are,
a flame, a light, a pure divine soul,
all as One.

It is in the realization of your Oneness,
our Oneness,

that forgiveness becomes your natural state of being.

PINE, OAK, NEST AND ROBIN

Immortal Pine, emanating grace and peace, standing tall
    and proud.
You can see the whimsey on her branches of needles and
    pine cones.
You can feel her joy as she dances and sways in the
    wind.
Her roots run deep into the darkness of the earth.
Meeting and intertwining with the roots of another.

Noble Oak stands as tall and twice as wide as her sister
    Pine.
You can see Oak's wisdom and knowledge evidenced on
    her thick long twisted branches.
You can feel her resilience and strength weathered on
    her bark.

Two beautiful trees.
Majestic in their own right.
Powerful, sturdy, steadfast.
Limbs and roots interlacing, touching, blending and
    sharing.

Together they stand in awe, reaching needles and leaves
    toward the sun and pure blue sky.
Together they bask in the moonlight and the expanse of
    the star filled universe.

Together they whisper and giggle at God's wonders, for
the ones that creep and crawl amongst their roots
and the ones that scamper and fly amongst their
branches.
Together they provide the food and material to stay
nourished and protected, a home to find rest and
shelter.

Nests of all varieties, large and small, are sprinkled amid
Pine and Oaks treetops.
Gray, bushy tailed, squirrels scamper up and around
Oaks wide truck onto Pines branches and back over
to Oak again.
A tightrope of balance and dexterity as the squirrels run
and play.
Birds of all varieties, chickadees, blue jays, sparrows,
robins and cardinals, perch throughout the
branches.
Their bird song, a melody, rising together as a sweet
chorus of gleeful exultation.

There is a small nest, high above, in Pine.
A nest made of her needles and bits of twine and string,
twigs and old leaves from Oak,
All carefully, beautifully, intricately placed together with
mud.
A nest of beginnings, a nest to hold and nurture new life.

A fledgling, a young Robin, feels safe in her nest built
with love and intuition.
It is her home, her protection, her sustenance.

Robin begins to feel the pull and hear the whispers deep
inside of something more.

An urging of flight and the promise of truth tickles her
ears.

She doesn't want to leave her safe home and the nest
made of trees.

It is all Robin has ever known.

Pine begins to rock and move in the wind, dropping her
pine cones and nuts.

Oak begins to rustle her branches in the breeze, releasing
her acorns and leaves.

Gentle urges from Pine and Oak insisting to Robin it is
time to fly.

Time to spread her wings.

To discover what lies beyond.

To discover the beauty and the power of what lies
within.

Tentatively, insecure, nervous even, but so strongly sure
this must be right and true.

Robin spreads her tiny wings.

She steps to the edge of her nest, her warm and safe
shelter.

She releases her fear, closes her eyes, and takes a deep
breath.

Pine softly encourages, "Spread your wings, Brave One."

Oak tenderly offers her wisdom, "Trust your soul and
fly."

Robin flaps her wings once.

Twice.

Three times.

And steps over the edge.

Freefalling at first until she remembers something inside
of her, a flicker of light, a blurry and distant
memory, to flap harder and harder, stronger and
more sure than ever.

Robin gains speed.

Climbing higher into the air.

Faster and faster.

She begins to soar.

Finding home and wholeness in the vastness of the sky.

Free.

Robin circles above her beloved trees in thanksgiving.

Pine and Oak bow their branches in humble gratitude.

For any tree can hold a nest, but they were the ones
chosen.

They were the ones to lend their shelter and food.

To share their wisdom and strength.

And to bear witness to a tiny bird trusting her soul.

Pine and Oak return attention back to the gentle breeze,
the sun and the stars beyond.

And continue to sway together.

VESSEL

I am a vessel.
Words, thoughts, ideas, creations
all pour through me.
They are not of me.
Nor are they mine to keep.
What flows through me is of the Divine.
What pours out of me is for all others.
I claim nothing.
For there is nothing of my own to claim.

I am a vessel.
It is enough to have been chosen as the vessel for this
    work.
For these words.
For these ideas.
I am not the only vessel.
There are many.
We are all vessels of a sort.
As we are all the same.

I am a vessel.
One amongst the shelves.
Rows upon rows, from floor to ceiling of shelves filling
    the cosmos.
As many as there are stars in the universe there are

vessels of all varieties.

Some as sturdy stoneware, unglazed and substantial, with
   wide thick handles.

Others as porcelain, dainty and elegant, hand painted
   with intricate design.

Still others tall and skinny, some short and stout.

Several as petite or bulky, ethereal or robust.

Plenty show signs of wear, a few chipped along the rim.

All perfect in their functioning.

All created unique and different by the Divine

All created with the same infinite love that is the Divine.

I am a vessel.

Divine Love and Light pour out of me.

As it is Divine Love and Light that God Source pours
   into me.

BUBBLES

Big
Tiny
Oblong or a perfectly round sphere
Iridescent
Shimmery
Flowing
Transforming
Graceful
Drifting
Floating with the breeze
Up
Up
Up to the multiverses

How can one not smile at the beauty and wonder of a
    marvelously formed bubble?
Pure happiness
And delight felt
When gazing at the abundant joy a bubble exudes
Unassuming
No expectations
No agenda
Content with being
A reminder of our authentic self

Could it be that God Source looks at us this way?
Is it possible to live free and joyous as a bubble?
Magnificently created
Light reflective
Moving with the winds
Free

And when the journey is done
A gentle pop
A burst of expansion
Back to God Source

FRACTURE

Break open.
Allow yourself to break apart.
Oh! I know it hurts, Dear One.
Hold my hand.
Squeeze it tight.
Break open
and be free.

YOUR ANGER

Imagine a pebble, a small rock, stuck in your shoe.
Imagine you notice it.
It's annoying, you are aware it's there,
but it's not something you think to stop and remove.

Now imagine you walking a mile with that pebble stuck
    in your shoe.
It's giving you some discomfort.
It might even rub your foot a little bit creating a blister.

Now walk two miles, or five, or fifty with the pebble still
    stuck in your shoe.
It hurts.
Thoughts keep coming back to it.
The place it rubbed on your foot is now raw, red and
    inflamed.
Maybe the skin has broken.
Maybe the dirt of the pebble and of your sock and shoe
    are now getting into the open flesh,
irritating it even more.

And now, you cannot ignore the pebble any longer,
it has your full attention.
You are forced to sit down and to remove your shoe and
    the offensive pebble.

You are forced to care for your now festering wound.
So that your foot may be healed,
so that you may walk again in your shoes.

So too, with anger, Dear One.

You can try and ignore your anger.
But only for a time,
before it begins to fester and create a wound within you
    that is deep and bloody and raw,
before you are forced to tend to that anger.

And as with the pebble,
the anger must be realized first,
then removed,
and lastly, the wound on the heart must be healed.

The anger must be realized and felt, acknowledged and
    learned from.
It comes as a lesson, as a way to remember a deeper
    truth about yourself.
The anger must be plucked out of your being and cast
    away, lovingly released with gratitude.
Similar to how you would pluck the pebble out of your
    shoe thankful it is no longer there.
Your wound that the anger rubbed onto your heart must
    be nurtured, cared for, and loved back to wholeness.
By forgiving yourself, loving yourself, showing grace and
    patience with yourself.

Anger is not the truth of who we are.

Just as the pebble in your shoe is a nuisance,
and not something you walk with forever,
so too, anger is a nuisance,
it is an emotion, a feeling,
to be realized, felt, learned from
and then released.

Our true essence is wholeness and Oneness.
And no matter how many times you might find that
    pebble of anger in your shoe and on your heart,
wholeness can be remembered again and again.

Stop ignoring the anger.
Realize it, feel it, release it .
And tend to your heart,
remembering the Divine Truth of who you are as One.

TAPESTRY

Warp, the vertical threads of a tapestry.
Weft, the horizontal fibers spanning across a weaving.
Are woven together
over under, over under,
Rhythmic. Pulse-like.
Interconnecting.

The warp cannot be held on its own without the weft.
The weft cannot keep on its own without the warp.

The warp is our sameness.
The weft is our lessons,
our individual journeys.

The warp is our soul.
Our spirit.
What we have in common with every other human here.
That is, we are divine souls of infinite love and light.
We all chose to be here during this time,
to come into a human body with a beating heart.

The weft is our own personal story.
Our own life journey.
Sacred experiences full of lessons
that bring feelings of intense heartache and immense joy,

fears that we strive to let go of, and love that we feel so
    deeply.

All of this, woven together with a golden strand of light.
A Light that forever flickers within us.
Reminding us of our I AM.
Our Wholeness.
Our Oneness.

No two tapestries look alike, just as no two lives look
    alike.
Yet we are connected,
we have the same makeup as warp threads, we are the
    same at our center, at our essence.
No matter what our weaving looks like, the light is the
    same within all of us
regardless of what we have been through, regardless of
    the weft colors chosen, the textures we may or may
    not have added to our life's tapestry.
We are the same at our core.

Oftentimes we don't see the magnificence of our
    tapestry,
or the tapestry of another.
It is not until we take a step back,
finally seeing the cohesiveness,
we begin to understand how all parts have become a
    whole.
Basking in our knowing of our sameness,
honoring all stories,

and remembering our golden strand of light woven throughout.

We can then stare in awe and wonderment at the beauty of our life.

The way God Source stares at us in awe and wonderment.

As perfect, breathtakingly exquisite, full of color and texture, all unique, and yet the same.

Woven together as One into a glorious tapestry.

THE QUEEN

Trusting her inner knowing,
she sends out the call and signals it is time to leave and
  find a new home.
Humbled with gratitude for the ones that have answered
and are willing to travel with her on a journey.
A voyage in search of new shelter, new beginnings, new
  life.
She knows it is time to split leaving the familiar behind,
  food and brood of beloved babies.
Time for another to reign,
for another to step into her role.

She feels the weight of responsibility upon her back.
But can no longer ignore the soft whisper of more.
The promise of what might lie beyond
dispels any hesitation she may have.
She says her goodbye, trusts that all will be well, and
  doesn't look back
as she flies out fearlessly into the next chapter of her
  expansion.

The honeybees swarm around her.
A helicopter buzz of flight and flurry filling the air.
Flying in controlled chaos,
in a smooth and guided flight.

The ones closest to her fly as an escort to the resting
    place.
Even more daughters surround.
Protecting, tending,
exchanging love energy with her and their sisters.
All trusting in her wisdom.
Savoring her nurturing love and guidance.
All willing to follow her call,
to fly blindly, leaving the familiar to venture into the
    unknown.

Scouts sent ahead.
Home space found.
A march inside to discover and familiarize with their new
    abode.
She settles in quickly beginning her work,
signaling her daughters where to build the comb and the
    brood nest.
All efforts are put forth to construct quickly and
    accurately.
Water, nectar, pollen foraged.
Life giving food subsistence.
New eggs laid.
All is settled.
All is well.

She is pleased with her new home,
a beautiful space full of potential and hope.
She leans in and can feel the pulse of the hive beating
    strong.
The buzz and hum is a soothing and familiar vibration.

Connected to all of the vibrations sharing a home on
    Earth mother.
The same vibration as the Source Creator.
A soft and gentle buzz of sacred life.

CURRENT

Surrender to the flow.
The great big, beautiful, mysterious flow of the universe.

Just as an oceans current is unseen,
and only felt,
the flow of the universe is rarely known and understood.

You can choose to go against the current.
Demanding and commanding your life to go in a certain
    direction,
with certain people,
controlling others and events,
resisting the lessons that flow your way.

Or, you can choose to surrender.

Fighting against the current will bring you nowhere.
Surrendering to the current is the only way home.

Lay down your fight,
accept the love and flow of the universe.
Release yourself to the perfect and divine current of your
    life's journey
knowing that when surrender happens,

you float with the current to exactly where you need to
    be.
Trusting that all circumstances,
all experiences,
all people
are for your highest good.

Remember that you are held,
supported and
free.

TRANSITION

Transition for some is so easy.
A seamless and smooth flow.
For others, it seems as if the world is ending.
A frightful force of change and loss of control.

Listen close, Dear One.
Come in, nearer to my heart.
Feel my love for you and remember the truth I speak
when I say, there is nothing to fear.
You are fully supported and never alone.

Transition is necessary.
Necessary to make room for the possibility of something
    more.
Something better and greater than what can be imagined.

Transition is the releasing of the old to make room for
    the new.
Not tossing away the old.
No, on the contrary,
it is the honoring of the becoming that has already
    occurred.
The honoring of the previous lessons learned
and experiences had.
Then allowing there to be room for more.

Something fresh.
Something profound,
exciting and true.
Transforming you more fully into the beautiful Light
that you are.

Turn your head to the sun, Dear One.
Gaze up.
Outstretch your arms and raise your palms high.
Whisper in your heart-
"I am ready.
I am ready for the transition, for the change.
For the more.
For the unexplored.
For the not yet learned or discovered yet.
I am ready for the expansion of what it is to come.
I look fearlessly forward.
Thankful for what lies behind.
Humbled for what is to come."

Step into and transition from the before into the now.
The only and forever

Now.

TO NURTURE

What does it mean to nurture?
To nurture yourself? Your partner? Your children or
    older parents?
To nurture the sky?
The land?
The sea?
Nurture the tiny creatures?
The large predators?

What does it mean to nurture?
Is it pampering yourself or cooking a meal for another?
Is it protecting the wildlife, the most vulnerable or ones
    without a voice?
Is it giving extra hugs?
Or providing shelter and sanctuary for those in need?

Is it possible to nurture some and not all?
Or is it automatic that if you nurture one, you nurture
    all?

Who are the nurtures?
Is it in all of us to nurture?
Or a select few?
Is it learned or does it come instinctively?
Does one aspire to be a nurturer?

Or to be nurtured?

I know this....

To nurture is to simply Love.
It is impossible to nurture one and not all.
For when you Know yourself and Love yourself, you
    Love all.
And Love is the essence,
the sustenance,
the purpose of life.

To all of those needing a nurturing rest, I invite you to
    come.
Gather close and lean in Dear One, feel my heart wrap
    you in glowing Love.
It matters not who you are or where you come from.
    What you have or don't have. What you have done
    or aspire to still do. What you look like or act like.
All.
All are invited.
My arms are forever outstretched.
My hands are forever open to receive you.
My heart is forever shining pure love and light into
    yours.
Come, let me nurture you whole again.

SYMPHONY OF SUMMER

During the late afternoon light,
as the sun burns low in the sky
kissing the land,
long and scorched shadows dance in the haze.

Have you ever just sat and listened
noticing the sounds that surround you
and tickle your ears?

Do you hear your heartbeat,
the steady rhythm that is you?
What about your breath?
Have you noticed the swoosh of inhale and release of
    exhale?
What about the space between your breaths?
That fleeting second of silence.
Do you hear it?

Have you listened to the cicadas singing and the
    mourning doves calling?
Can you hear the ant crunch the leaf as it travels home?
Or the buzz of the bee visiting one more flower,
    insatiable in the taste of nectar.

It all becomes a symphony of summer,

of the heat
and moisture laden air.
Calling, back and forth,
lamenting.
Sounding the vibration of life.
Reminding of their presence,
and their place among all.
A crescendo echoing through the trees.

Then, a fleeting moment
of silence
before it begins again.

It is in this space between,
that quick second
of quiet,
where peace resides.

MUCHNESS

Do not believe the world when they tell you that you are
    'too much'.
There is no such thing as 'too much'.

You are you.
Unique and perfect.
There is no other you,
but you.

Be 'too much'.
Be too loud,
too quiet,
too big,
too flighty
with your head in the clouds.
Be too scattered,
too energetic.
Be too serious
or too creative,
or too outgoing,
or too shy.

You are not 'too much' of anything.

You are the perfect portion of everything.

Stand strong,
resolute in your thoughts and desires.
Don't bow down.
You are not 'too much'.

Your muchness is what is needed to change this world.
To pioneer a new way of thinking,
being and
seeing.
To usher in even more pure Light and Love.

Your muchness is what shines so brightly,
adds sparkle to your eyes.
It is your soul shining through that is free and can never
be tamed or caged.

Be too much, Dear One.
You have permission.

THE WIND

Close your eyes,
become still.
Feel the wind.

Feel the breeze, so soft and tender,
caressing your face.
Enveloping you in a flutter of leaves falling.
Blowing cool and graceful.

You can feel the angels on the breeze,
their sweet wings brushing past your cheek,
your arms,
leaving their tingling caress behind
and whispering their forever presence.

Oh, how I cherish the wind.
The rustling, the movement and the gentleness.
Releasing the old and making way for the new.

A leaf meanders to the ground,
swaying this way, and that,
whirling,
slow at first
then sure.
So serene.
Peaceful.
Carefree.

Let the winds of transformation carry you like the leaf.
Floating and completely supported.

Let the angels spiral and twirl around you.
Reach out.
Believe,
and feel them near.
Listen and know their soft songs of hope and love.

Let the breeze take you back.
Back to your origin, to where you came from.

Allow yourself to remember the lightness.
Allow yourself to remember your authentic soul dancing
in the wind,
surrounded by the angels,
joyous,
light,
blissful,
and free.

THE CALLING

Come back.
Come back to me, my beloved.
Come back to the stillness and silence found within the
    wooded forest of your heart.
Come back to the wild exuberant conversation that is us.

I have missed you so.
And have longed for your presence once again.

Tread softly on my beating and raw heart.
I have shown you all.
Shared all.
Bared everything.
I have opened myself to your sweet fragrance of nectar
    and sweat.
And have been left with the lingering scent of heavenly
    decay.

Come back to me.
To us.
You remember the way.

I will be awaiting your return
with open arms and a tender caress.

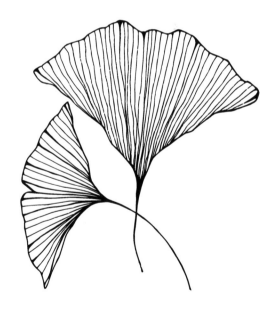

ABOUT THE AUTHOR

Amanda L. Bohmont's creative journey began as a young child when art became a passion of hers as she found solace in creating. She went on to get her degree in Art Education and Studio Art from the University of West Florida. She has taught art for a number of years, both in the classroom and out, to young children, adolescents, and adults. Amanda creates pottery and glass mosaics, weavings and fiber art. Recently, she has picked up a paintbrush.

She draws her inspiration from nature and craves being outside under the blue sky and warmth of the sunshine. Intentionally meandering through the woods, listening to the sounds of nature, noticing the small creatures, and talking to trees brings her great peace and joy. She has a thriving vegetable garden where she grows food for her family, and she's a certified beekeeper.

Amanda is a Practitioner of Healing Arts and a facilitator in The Vistara School. She is also the Co-Creator of CreativeSoul, a branch of The Vistara School, offering soulful art workshops. Creating meaningful art workshops and acting as a guide to others through their own creative art process and journey fulfills Amanda's soul's calling and passion for serving others and teaching.

She lives just outside of Charlotte, NC with her husband, five earth-side children and an ever-present Emmett in spirit, savoring each moment in surrender to Divine Flow.

Made in the USA
Columbia, SC
17 October 2022

69528396R00067